Donated to the Alameda County Library

Fremont Cultural Arts Council

in support of fine arts education for the young
people of our community

21st
Century
Skills Library

COOL ARTS CAREERS

SPECIAL EFFECTS TECHNICIAN

MATT MULLINS

CHERRY LAKE Publishing

Published in the United States of America by
Cherry Lake Publishing, Ann Arbor, Michigan
www.cherrylakepublishing.com

Content Adviser
Linda Siegel, Senior Training Manager, Digital Domain, Venice, California.

Special thanks to John Andrew Berton Jr., an independent visual effects supervisor,
and Jennifer Emberly, visual effects supervisor and cofounder of Atomic Fiction.

Credits
Cover and page 1, ©iStockphoto.com/mikespics; page 4, ©Pictorial Press Ltd/
Alamy; page 6, ©Faizzaki/Dreamstime.com; page 9, ©Hemis/Alamy; page 10,
page 15, and page 16, ©AF archive/Alamy; page 12, ©Jeff Greenberg/Alamy;
page 13, ©Scott Tucker/Alamy; pages 14 and 28, ©Moviestore collection
Ltd/Alamy; page 15, © photolibrary. All rights reserved; page 19, ©Jeff Morgan
01/Alamy; page 20, ©Greenland/Dreamstime.com; page 23, ©Mary Evans Picture
Library/Alamy; page 24, ©Photos 12/Alamy; page 26, ©James Blinn/Dreamstime.com

Library of Congress Cataloging-in-Publication Data
Mullins, Matt.
  Special effects technician/by Matt Mullins.
    p. cm.—(Cool arts careers)
  Includes bibliographical references and index.
  ISBN-13: 978-1-61080-134-8 (lib. bdg.)
  ISBN-10: 1-61080-134-2 (lib. bdg.)
  1. Cinematography—Special effects—Vocational guidance—Juvenile literature.
  2. Motion picture industry—Vocational guidance—Juvenile literature. I. Title.
  TR858.M95 2012
  778.5'345023—dc22   2011002474

Cherry Lake Publishing would like to acknowledge
the work of The Partnership for 21st Century Skills.
Please visit *www.21stcenturyskills.org* for more information.

Printed in the United States of America
Corporate Graphics, Inc.
July 2011
CLFA09

TABLE OF CONTENTS

CHAPTER ONE
FILM MAGICIANS

The film *Harry Potter and the Half-Blood Prince* features a **scene** in which ghostly shapes attack as people cross a bridge in London. The bridge twists, turns, and crashes into the water below.

A team of special effects technicians helped make the movie Gladiator *starring Russell Crowe.*

Filmmakers did not really destroy the bridge. Instead, they used **computer graphics** to make the bridge look like it was falling apart. This is one example of special effects. Special effects make impossible things happen on screen. They can involve big things like destroying bridges or small things like changing an actor's eye color. These effects are created by workers called special effects technicians.

There are many kinds of special effects. Some actually happen during filming. One example might be a small explosion that a technician sets off. A camera operator shoots the explosion on film. This kind of effect is sometimes called a **special mechanical effect**.

Explosions are a common special effect in action movies. Special effects technicians plan the explosions carefully. They make the object they are blowing up extra weak in some spots. This helps them make sure the pieces will fly in the right directions. They also make sure that actors standing near the explosion will not be hurt.

Special visual effects happen off camera. This means they are added to the film after a scene is shot. In the movie *Gladiator*, the main character fights in a giant stadium. The crowd roars when one of the fighters is hurt. Most of the crowd and the stadium were added using computer graphics after the action was shot.

Gunshots in movies are also special effects. Imagine a movie hero running through a door as bullets smash into the doorway.

A special effects technician sets up this shot by cutting away a piece of the door. He puts in a tiny **charge** that is controlled electronically. Then he places the cut wood back in its spot. Paint and fillers are used to make the doorway look untouched. The technician makes the charge explode at the right moment. It looks like a bullet has hit the door and chipped a piece off. But it exploded inside the door.

The **Transformer** *films used special effects to create the Transformer characters, including Bumblebee.*

Makeup and creature effects are also created by special effects technicians. Big monsters like the ones in *Aliens* or *Predator* are made using costumes that combine **prosthetics** with monster suits and makeup. Some costumes even use robotic puppetry. These robotics make body parts such as tails or wings move around.

Weather effects are also common in many movies. Storms are created with giant fans and huge water hoses. Snowstorms are made with snow machines like the ones at ski resorts. Miniature effects use small models of cities or vehicles. They are filmed to look life-size. Miniature cities are built so they can be destroyed by floods or alien attacks. Today, some weather and miniature effects are done entirely on computers.

Special effects also correct problems after the film is shot. A director reviewing **footage** for his new Western might notice that there is a stop sign in one shot. Visual effects technicians fix the image by taking the sign out. Maybe the director thinks a scene has too much blue in it. A special effects technician can correct the color.

Almost every movie made today uses special effects. If the technicians do their jobs well, you won't notice that the effects are there. John Andrew Berton Jr. works on special effects for Hollywood movies, such as the 2008 comedy *Bedtime Stories*. In one scene from that movie, the characters are in a skyscraper. The director wanted the scene

LEARNING & INNOVATION SKILLS

One of the very first special effects technicians was a magician. Georges Méliès owned a theater in Paris where he performed magic shows. He saw a movie for the first time in 1895. This inspired him to buy a movie camera and make his own films.

Méliès made more than 500 films by 1914! His 1902 movie *A Trip to the Moon* had amazing special effects for its time. It featured a moon with a moving face. The face even begins to cry when a rocket ship crashes into it.

to take place on the top floor of a skyscraper. But the middle floors of other skyscrapers were visible behind the actors. Special visual effects technicians fixed this after filming. They digitally replaced the skyscrapers with clear sky. This made it look like the actors were way up high instead of down on the middle floors!

Watch the film and you probably won't be able to tell. That's because Berton and the other technicians did their jobs so well. Like good magicians, special effects technicians make it hard to notice their tricks.

Méliès created alien creatures called Selenites for A Trip to the Moon.

CHAPTER TWO
A DAY ON THE JOB

Think about the movie *Jurassic Park*. Its director, Steven Spielberg, is well known for his use of special effects. He used giant dinosaur puppets in some scenes. Other scenes featured computer-generated creatures.

Special effects allowed actor Sam Neill to run with a flock of dinosaurs in Jurassic Park.

Computer-generated creatures are very common in today's movies. Actors pretend to run away or scream in terror at something that isn't actually there when the camera is running. In *The Lord of the Rings: The Fellowship of the Ring*, actor Ian McKellen faces off against a giant, flaming demon. In real life, he was shouting at a tennis ball hung from up high!

Effects such as dinosaurs and flaming monsters must look like they are really there with the actors. Making this happen is a very complicated job. It takes many special effects technicians to keep track of where the actor is in a shot, how the actor moves, and how the monster should move. They must also pay attention to the lighting conditions and where the actor's eyes are looking. Most films have special effects supervisors in charge of this process.

John Andrew Berton Jr. was a special effects supervisor on *Charlotte's Web*. This is a movie version of the classic E. B. White story about a barnyard pig and a spider who become friends. Berton's days began very early. He went to the movie **set** and checked his equipment to make sure it all worked. He turned on the computers and got everything going for the technicians.

Then Berton met with the film's director to talk about the day ahead. They discussed the shooting schedule. Then they discussed details of the special effects in each shot. They figured out where actors should stand in scenes and where other characters would be added later with effects.

Actors often act on simple sets with large green or blue screens behind them. The screens are later replaced with computer-generated backgrounds. Berton and the director discussed lighting for those scenes. They even talked about what the reflections in a character's eyes should look like!

Details like this require a lot of planning. Technicians need information from each scene to make their effects look real. Berton made sure all the necessary information was gathered.

Maps and other images in weather reports are usually created using a green screen.

The walls in this set serve as a green screen for special effects to be added.

He also made sure that the **data** was sent to the right technicians. He sent information from a shoot in Australia to a technician in California. This allowed the technician to do his part of the work.

Sometimes the weather would change during the day. The shooting schedule had to be adjusted. They would have to shoot different scenes than the ones they planned. Berton made sure all the special effects data was saved correctly. He also made sure the data was gathered correctly for the new scenes that weren't originally planned for the day.

The special effects supervisor has to stay up-to-date with what the director has planned.

Special effects can take a lot of preparation before filming starts.

Filming takes several months for most movies. Most special visual effects are made after all the filming is done. Jennifer Emberly is a special effects technician who worked with Berton on *The Mummy*. She was also director of **animation** on *A Christmas Carol*. This computer-animated film required a lot of special effects work. Digital characters in movies such as *The Mummy* and *A Christmas Carol* are created using **motion capture**. This allows special effects technicians to create animated characters that move like real people.

LIFE & CAREER SKILLS

Made-up creatures move just like real people in movies like *The Mummy* or *Avatar*. Special effects technicians use motion capture to make this happen. Actors wear body suits covered with special sensors that look like Ping-Pong balls. Special cameras record the suits' movements by bouncing lights off the sensors.

Technicians use the recorded motion of the real actors to create the motion of animated creatures on the computer. The animated characters are then put into the filmed scene. Technicians work day after day until they look just right. Each character can take many weeks of work to create.

Actor Brendan Fraser fights off unfinished animated mummies in The Mummy.

Emberly started her days early when she worked on *A Christmas Carol.* She met with visual effects supervisors, animators, people who worked with creature suits, and others. They talked about deadlines and decided which scenes to focus on. They set schedules and tried to solve any problems they were having.

In some scenes, a character's hair wasn't looking quite right. Emberly worked with animators to fix the problem. Later that morning, she watched **dailies** with animation teams. They watched scenes over and over to look for mistakes. They looked closely at each character's movements. Emberly helped the animators make any necessary changes.

Emberly spent afternoons working with individual animators. She looked at their work and talked with them about how to handle certain scenes. She often went to more meetings later in the day. Sometimes she met with the director or other people working on the film. Each day required a lot of discussion. The effects team made adjustments to even the smallest details. Animated and live action films rely on special effects technicians to make even the most unusual things look perfectly real.

Animators must pay close attention to design and movement.

CHAPTER THREE
BECOMING A SPECIAL EFFECTS TECHNICIAN

I f you would like to create special effects someday, you can start by watching a lot of movies! The next thing you

You can experiment with creating special effects in your own movies.

should do is borrow a camera and make movies of your own. Try out effects. Get an idea of how movies are made.

You don't have to study special effects in college. Instead, study something else that you enjoy. Do you like to build things or take things apart? Take classes in mechanical engineering and physics. Maybe you like to draw. Take art classes, animation classes, and design classes. Take theater classes and learn to do makeup. You can also learn to build sets or work with lights.

Learn to use computers well. Play with photo and moviemaking software. Do whatever you enjoy, but keep moviemaking in mind. Special effects technicians work with many different materials. Some do makeup and prosthetics. Some create robotic devices. Others edit photography or design characters on their computers. All of them work with computers.

Learn to notice and solve problems. Study how things move and look in the real world. Try to figure out how moviemakers created the effects in your favorite movies. Watch the special features on DVDs and Blu-ray Discs that take you behind the scenes.

One of the exciting things about making movies is that you can explore anything you are interested in. Emberly created skeleton-like mummies for *The Mummy*. She remembers how she placed the creepy-looking creatures in scenes with live actors. "It fit really nicely together," she explained. "I was really intrigued by the possibilities."

That's what led her to work more with motion capture. She founded a brand-new visual effects company. If you study what interests you and learn a variety of skills, you could work some movie magic of your own!

LEARNING & INNOVATION SKILLS

It takes creative thinking to come up with special effects. One of the first special effects that was developed is known as Pepper's Ghost. This trick has been used to make fake ghosts appear since it was invented by Professor John Henry Pepper in the 1860s.

The effect uses two rooms. One room is the one the audience sees. The other is a mirror image of the first room. A special mirror is set up between the rooms. In the secret room, a light shines on an actor dressed as a ghost. The light shines through the special mirror onto the stage. This causes a ghost to appear onstage. Audiences were very surprised when they first saw this happen!

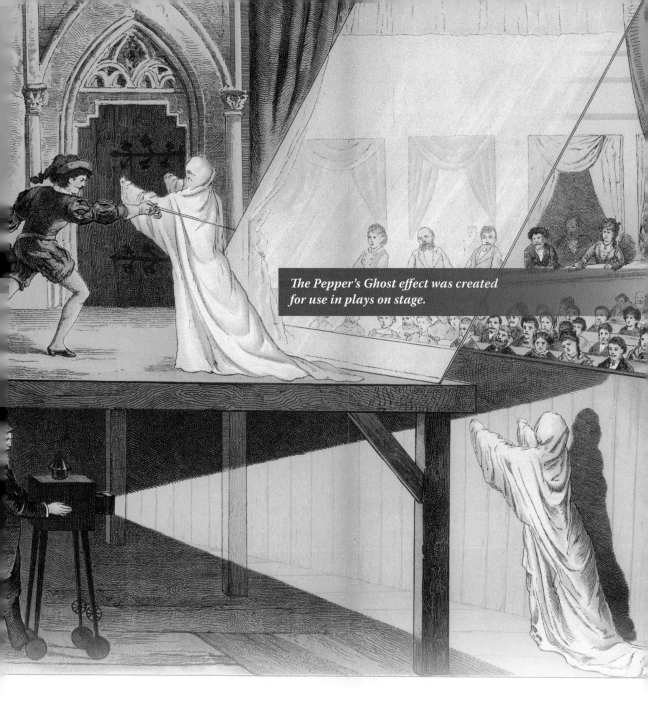

The Pepper's Ghost effect was created for use in plays on stage.

CHAPTER FOUR
SPECIAL EFFECTS IN THE FUTURE

Technology continues to change. People come up with new ways to use computers and other devices. Special effects change, too. James Cameron is one director who is well known for creating amazing special effects.

James Cameron gives directions to actor Sam Worthington on the Avatar *set.*

Cameron shot his 2009 film *Avatar* using a new three-dimensional (3-D) camera system. His system included two cameras in one device. This gave the effect of viewing with two eyes like people do in real life. He was able to capture every shot from two slightly different angles. This allowed special effects technicians to create a lifelike 3-D image. In the movie's alien world, it sometimes looks like branches or tiny creatures are coming right off the screen!

The blue Na'vi aliens in the movie were animated characters based closely on real actors. Cameron invented

21ST CENTURY CONTENT

New technology brings new ways to watch movies, television shows, and other videos. Filmmakers today often create projects with extra videos that can be watched on phones, tablet computers, and YouTube.

Special effects people find themselves creating many kinds of videos when they are hired to work on a movie. Sometimes they create short animations based on one of the movie's characters. These projects draw attention to the movie they are based on. They help make a movie more popular and successful.

a new way to record facial expressions for these animated characters. This helped animators create realistic face movement. Actors' faces were covered with little dots. The dots acted like the sensors on motion capture body suits. The actors also wore helmets with small cameras attached. These cameras recorded changes in the actors' facial muscles. Special effects technicians used this data to create the Na'vis' facial expressions. It was another step forward for motion capture effects.

More movies are being made with 3-D effects, which require special glasses to watch.

Avatar was not the first movie to use motion capture. Other movies have used this kind of effect for one or two characters that weren't in the movie much. But *Avatar* used special visual effect characters for most of the movie. The most impressive part is that most of these characters spoke. Faces with moving mouths are among the hardest things to animate realistically. This is because mouths and faces have many muscles that move in complicated ways.

LEARNING & INNOVATION SKILLS

New types of movie screens are changing the way we watch movies. 3-D movies add depth to the picture. The special glasses we wear make it look like things are coming right off the screen.

Some theaters add equipment to seats to make them shake, spray water for flood scenes, or even create smells for certain scenes. This is called 4-D. Can you think of things that you could do in a theater that would make 4-D even more realistic? How could you make movie watchers feel like they are really in the movie?

Computer animation techniques will continue to grow and change. One thing that has not been done yet is creating characters that look perfectly human. Faces, skin, and human movement remain very difficult to re-create with effects. *Avatar* did a great job with the Na'vi, but they were alien characters. "The next big challenge," says Emberly, "is to try to duplicate a human being."

*Avatar **won awards for its special effects.***

SOME FAMOUS SPECIAL EFFECTS TECHNICIANS

Ray Harryhausen (1920–) is one of the most successful special effects technicians in movie history. He worked with Willis O'Brien on *Mighty Joe Young* (1949) and later created effects for movies like *The 7th Voyage of Sinbad* (1958) and *Jason and the Argonauts* (1963). These films include famous effects such as sword fights between men and skeletons. The last film he worked on was *Clash of the Titans* (1981).

John Knoll (1962–) created the popular Adobe Photoshop photo-editing software with his brother, Thomas. He later worked as visual effects supervisor on the *Star Wars* prequels, all three *Pirates of the Caribbean* films, and *Avatar*. He won an Academy Award for *Pirates of the Caribbean: Dead Man's Chest* (2006).

Dennis Muren (1946–) has won eight Academy Awards for his effects work in movies such as *The Abyss* (1989), *Terminator 2: Judgment Day* (1991), and *Jurassic Park* (1993). He has also worked on some of the *Star Wars* and *Indiana Jones* movies.

Willis O'Brien (1886–1962) was a cartoonist and sculptor before he began working on movies. He created the giant gorilla and dinosaur effects of the 1933 classic *King Kong*. It was one of the most famous early movies to use special effects.

Douglas Trumbull (1942–) worked on special photographic effects for many science fiction films. He worked with director Stanley Kubrick on *2001: A Space Odyssey* (1968). The film is widely considered one of the best ever made. Audiences were struck by its realistic scenes of space travel. The movie used cameras and projectors in new ways during filming.

GLOSSARY

animation (an-uh-MAY-shuhn) drawings or computer graphics that move, like a cartoon character

charge (CHARJ) an amount of explosive material

computer graphics (kuhm-PYOO-tuhr GRAFF-iks) images created with a computer rather than with a pen, paint, or other materials

dailies (DAY-leez) portions of a film shown on the same day they were shot

data (DAY-tuh) information

footage (FOO-tij) recorded film

motion capture (MOH-shuhn CAP-chur) using recorded movements to animate characters

prosthetics (pross-THET-iks) fake body parts

scene (SEEN) a small part of a larger story that takes place in a single location

set (SET) the location where a show or movie is filmed

special mechanical effect (SPESH-uhl muh-KAN-ik-uhl eff-EKT) an effect on film that actually happens

special visual effects (SPESH-uhl VIZH-oo-uhl eff-EKTS) effects that are added into a filmed scene

FOR MORE INFORMATION

BOOKS

Grabham, Tim. *Movie Maker.* Somerville, MA: Candlewick Press, 2010.

O'Brien, Lisa. *Lights, Camera, Action! Making Movies and TV from the Inside Out.* Toronto: Maple Tree Press, 2007.

Robins, Deri. *Special Effects.* London: QED, 2005.

WEB SITES

fxguide
www.fxguide.com
Check out behind-the-scenes interviews with special effects technicians.

How Stuff Works—Special Effects
entertainment.howstuffworks.com/special-effects-technology -channel.htm
Discover how special effects have been used in many different movies.

NOVA Online—Special Effects
www.pbs.org/wgbh/nova/specialfx/fxguide/
Enjoy some fun special effects activities.

INDEX

ABOUT THE AUTHOR

Matt Mullins lives in Madison, Wisconsin, with his son and writes about engineering, business strategy, design, and other topics. Formerly a journalist, Matt has written more than 20 children's books, and has written and directed three short films.